The Maya Civilization

LOUISE SPILSBURY

 raintree

a Capstone company — publishers for children

Raintree is an imprint of Capstone Global Library Limited, a company incorporated in England and Wales having its registered office at 264 Banbury Road, Oxford, OX2 7DY – Registered company number: 6695582

www.raintree.co.uk
myorders@raintree.co.uk

Original illustrations © Capstone Global Library Limited 2020
Originated by Capstone Global Library Ltd
Printed and bound in India

ISBN 978 1 4747 7776 6 (hardback)
ISBN 978 1 4747 7784 1 (paperback)

British Library Cataloguing in Publication Data
A full catalogue record for this book is available from the British Library.

Acknowledgements
We would like to thank the following for permission to reproduce photographs: Cover: Shutterstock: Diego Grandi: bottom; Deborah McCague: top; Inside: Shutterstock: AAR Studio: pp. 28–29; Adalbert Dragon: p. 5br; Ahau1969: pp. 4–5; Akarawut: p. 37br; Alpkhan Photography: p. 9br; Rafal Cichawa: p. 29br; Ernest2099: pp. 40–41; Frontpage: p. 33r; Diego Grandi: pp. 26–27; Meunierd: p. 45br; Milicenta: p. 13br; Nikidel: pp. 6–7; Mario Wong Pastor: p. 11br; David Pegzlz: p. 25; Dario Lo Presti: pp. 1, 24; Leon Rafael: pp. 8–9, 17r; Veleknez: p. 23br; Walters Art Museum: p. 35br; Wasanajai: p. 19br; Cezary Wojtkowski: pp. 27br, 30–31; Wikimedia Commons: Akubra: pp. 22–23; AlejandroLinaresGarcia: pp. 16–17; Peter Andersen: pp. 32–33; Daderot: pp. 12–13, 34–35; David at MARI: p. 39b; Dorieo: pp. 36–37; FA2010: pp. 20–21; Gift of Constance McCormick Fearing: p. 43r; Futons_of_rock: p. 15r; HJPD: p.41b; Infrogmation of New Orleans: pp. 14–15; Maly Kolezka: p. 21b; Salvador alc: pp. 38–39; Wolfgang Sauber: pp. 7r, 31br, 42–43; Pavel Vorobiev: pp. 44–45; Michel Wal: pp. 10–11; Wmpearl: pp. 18–19.

Every effort has been made to contact copyright holders of material reproduced in this book. Any omissions will be rectified in subsequent printings if notice is given to the publisher.

All the internet addresses (URLs) given in this book were valid at the time of going to press. However, due to the dynamic nature of the internet, some addresses may have changed, or sites may have changed or ceased to exist since publication. While the author and publisher regret any

Contents

CHAPTER 1

Blood and fear

The cities of the ancient Maya lay hidden in the jungles of Mexico and Central America for hundreds of years. When the ruins were found, they showed that the Mayan **civilization** was very advanced. The ruins also showed that it was built on blood and fear.

The **rainforests** where most Maya lived were filled with dangers. There were deadly biting insects, fierce pumas, sharp-toothed crocodiles and **venomous** snakes. The Maya also lived in fear of **evil spirits**. They believed that only their gods could protect them.

Tall temples reminded ordinary Maya that their fearsome gods were always watching them.

The Maya worshipped more than 150 different gods, most of which had a good and an evil side. They believed that to stay safe and successful, they had to offer their gods **sacrifices** of animal and human blood. They carried out these sacrifices at the top of their **temples**.

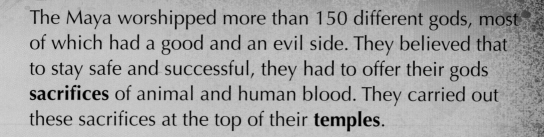

KILLER FACT!

The most feared animal in the Mayan world was the jaguar, the largest and most powerful cat in the Americas. This predator has razor-sharp claws and deadly fangs.

A jaguar can kill with one crushing bite to the skull.

Sinister cities

The first Maya were farmers who lived in small villages and towns. Gradually, power-hungry kings took control of whole areas. They ruled all the settlements around their large city strictly and sometimes unfairly.

The Maya built some cities and took over others left by previous ancient peoples. These cities were built on blood. For example, beneath a temple in Teotihuacán lay the bodies of headless animals and people sacrificed to make each layer of the pyramid **sacred** as it was built.

The king's palace and the temples where sacrifices were carried out lay in the centre of Mayan cities. The palaces were several stories high with courtyards, gardens and towers. But ordinary Mayan families lived in small, single-roomed, windowless houses on a platform of dirt to stop the rains from **flooding** them.

The main street through Teotihuacán was called the Avenue of the Dead.

6

DEADLY DID YOU KNOW?

The walls of Mayan cities were covered in carvings of gods and strange mythical creatures. These scary-looking creations kept ordinary people living in fear of the gods who ruled their lives.

This wall carving showing a scary mask is from the city of Placeres.

Bloody battles

Mayan kings regularly led their armies on bloodthirsty attacks against other cities. Warriors fought vicious battles day after day, until one side won.

These savage battles were fought so one city could win more land from another city, and to claim valuable treasures or goods. Kings also attacked other cities to capture enemies to use as **slaves** and for sacrifices. The **priests** who performed the sacrifices often told warriors when captives for sacrifice were needed.

Warriors fought battles only during the day. A battle continued until the leader of one army was hurt or killed. Then the losers had to pay a **tribute** to the winners. This tribute could include salt, textiles, gold, silver, copper and even people.

Mayan kings were constantly fighting vicious and bloodthirsty battles against each other.

DEADLY DID YOU KNOW?

Murderous Mayan warriors loved nothing more than capturing high-ranking enemies. These prisoners were taken home where they were humiliated and often murdered.

This stone **monument** to a king tells of his great success in ruthless battles.

CHAPTER 2

Macabre Maya

The Mayan kings were all-powerful. The royals and **nobles** took every chance they had to show off their wealth. They wore some **macabre** outfits to demonstrate how important they were.

Kings often wore skins of jaguars or other dangerous animals as a **symbol** of their power. Jaguars could sneak up on victims silently or leap on them suddenly from trees. They were seen as magical and terrifying, so kings thought people would fear them if they wore jaguar skins.

Kings and rich Maya covered their pots and walls with paintings of themselves wearing their fine clothes and headdresses.

Royals and nobles also wore headdresses made from hundreds of beautiful and valuable feathers plucked from rare birds, which they kept in cages. Some headdresses were taller than the people who wore them.

KILLER FACT!

Royals and nobles were the only people allowed to wear the long, bright-green tail feathers of the quetzal bird in their hair or headdresses. If an ordinary Maya wore feathers, their punishment could be death.

Quetzals were freed after their tail feathers were removed. The birds were sacred and the penalty for killing one was death.

Body modifications

Mayan kings and nobles not only wore macabre costumes, but they also modified (changed) the way they looked. The Maya believed that the more important a person was, the more extreme their body modifications should be.

The Maya thought that body modifications not only looked good, but were also a way to communicate with their gods. They believed their suffering and bleeding during these treatments were an exchange for the food, rain and life that the gods gave to them.

This warrior's facial scars would have been made by a knife cutting patterns into his skin.

Sometimes, kings, priests and nobles modified their teeth, too. They drilled holes into their teeth and then put pieces of precious stones such as jade, **obsidian** or turquoise into the holes.

KILLER FACT!

When the Maya went to war, warriors had their teeth filed into sharp points. This was not only a way to ask the gods for victory in war, but it also made the warriors look more ferocious to help them scare their enemies.

After a round hole was drilled into a tooth, a plug to fit it was cut from a lump of stone such as jade.

Faces of fear

The Maya's fear of their gods led them to take some desperate measures. They did all they could to please their gods, even changing the shape of their heads.

Some noble families tried to make their children look like the god of maize, who had a long, stretched head. They strapped boards to the front and back of a baby's head so that it would grow longer and thinner.

Some mothers hung a bead from the hair on their child's forehead so that it dangled permanently in front of their nose. This was meant to make the child cross-eyed. Parents did this to please and honour the sun god, who was shown as cross-eyed.

The Maya believed that reshaping their skulls not only brought them closer to the maize god, but also made them look more important.

KILLER FACT!

The Maya did not just use obsidian mirrors to check their appearance. Men looked into a mirror to show how brave they were. The Maya believed that evil creatures could reach through an obsidian mirror and drag them into the underworld.

A mirror-bearer, like this model of one, held up a mirror for the ruler to look at his reflection. A mirror was often aimed at a ruler when he was on his throne.

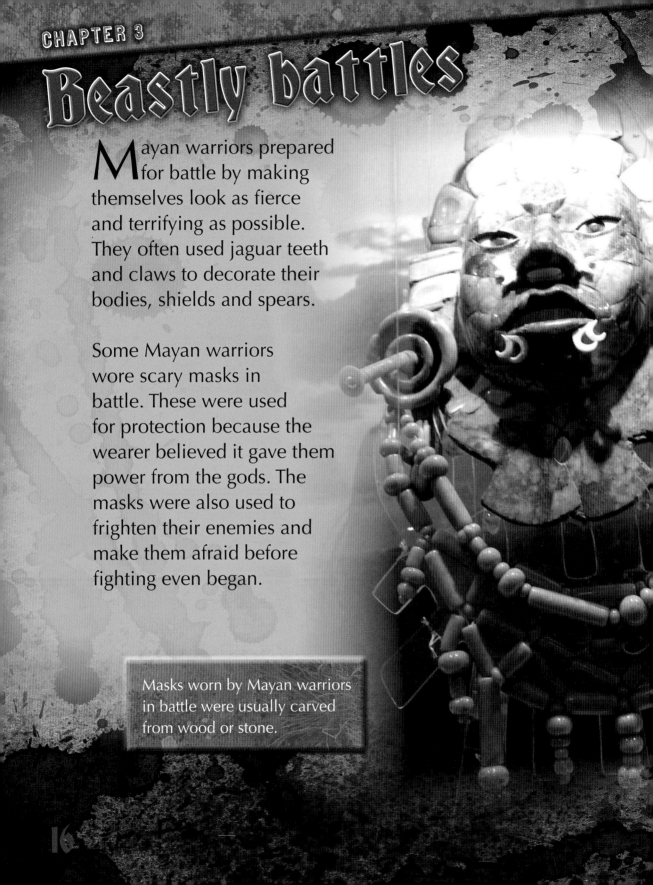

CHAPTER 3

Beastly battles

Mayan warriors prepared for battle by making themselves look as fierce and terrifying as possible. They often used jaguar teeth and claws to decorate their bodies, shields and spears.

Some Mayan warriors wore scary masks in battle. These were used for protection because the wearer believed it gave them power from the gods. The masks were also used to frighten their enemies and make them afraid before fighting even began.

Masks worn by Mayan warriors in battle were usually carved from wood or stone.

Warriors often had paintings or tattoos of animals such as snakes, eagles or jaguars on their face and body. These were some of the most dangerous animals in the Mayan world. Warriors wore images of these fearsome animals to show how important and deadly they were.

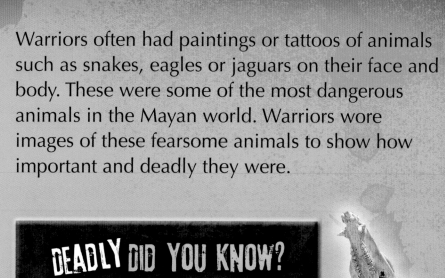

DEADLY DID YOU KNOW?
Some Mayan warriors are said to have worn a necklace made from the shrunken heads of enemies they had killed. This was to warn opponents just how dangerous they were.

Mayan warriors had tattoos on their skin. They were created by piercing the skin with needles. They believed this showed the gods that they were willing to suffer in order to honour them.

Menacing weapons

Mayan warriors charged at their enemies using a variety of vicious and deadly weapons. They also used **tear gas** and bombs to attack them.

Mayan warriors had stone weapons as well as weapons made of wood and shells. They fought with spears, slings, clubs, axes and knives. They carved obsidian rock into razor-sharp spear tips. They topped the arrows they shot from their bows with jagged fish teeth.

Mayan warriors carried shields that often had fierce faces carved into them to scare their enemies.

The Maya invented a type of tear gas. They burned large amounts of hot chillies to create a nasty smoke, which they blew towards the enemy. The thick, fiery smoke stung opponents' eyes and skin. While the enemies struggled to breathe and see, Mayan warriors attacked.

KILLER FACT!

The Maya made grenades using gourds, which are large fruits with a hard skin. They hollowed out the shell of the gourds and filled them with wasps and bees. Then they threw these grenades at their enemies.

The hole at the top of the gourd was filled with grass to keep the insects from escaping.

Suffering slaves

When Mayan warriors won a battle, they brought back captured enemies. Some of these prisoners of war became slaves. They were forced to work for the king, nobles, priests and farmers for free.

Slaves did all the worst jobs. They cleared routes through dangerous jungles and insect-infested swamps. Traders could then travel along these routes to buy and sell goods such as gold and jaguar skins. The slaves also had to carry these heavy goods long distances in large baskets on their backs.

This carving shows captives being presented to a ruler to become his slaves.

Slaves were forced to work on huge building projects such as temples and palaces. They carried stone and other materials on their backs or rolled them on logs from a **quarry** to the building site. Then they hacked away at the stone for many hours in the heat.

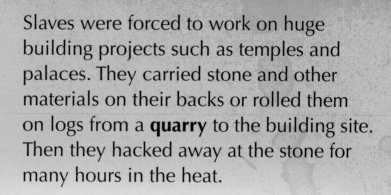

DEADLY DID YOU KNOW?

Some Maya became slaves as a form of punishment if they committed certain crimes or failed to pay what they owed. The poorest families sometimes sold a relative into slavery to make money.

The Maya made their slaves carve important symbols into stone. Some symbols, such as this one, showed the name of a Mayan ruler. His name was Great Jaguar Paw.

CHAPTER 4

Offerings of blood

The Maya believed that their gods controlled everything on Earth. If something bad happened, such as a violent storm, they thought the gods were angry with them. For the Maya, **offerings** of blood were the only way to keep the gods happy.

Bloodletting was the most common way that the Maya fed their ever-hungry gods with blood. They would cut themselves until they bled. Sometimes, a king used a knife or the sharp spine of a stingray to cut his skin and let the blood drop into a bowl.

This carved panel shows a bloodletting **ritual** in which a Mayan queen pulls a spiked rope through her tongue.

Bloodletting was also a way to speak to the gods in order to ask for their help. Sometimes, the blood released from the painful wound was used to soak paper. Then the paper was burned to send the blood and the people's prayers to the gods.

DEADLY DID YOU KNOW?
Some animals were sacrificed and their blood used as offerings to the gods. Animals such as turkeys, dogs, squirrels, lizards and crocodiles were sacrificed in great numbers.

Turkeys did not live long in Mayan times. The Maya used them for food or sacrificed them to their gods.

Scary sacrifices

The most important blood offerings came from human sacrifices. Human sacrifices took place in large numbers to celebrate a great victory in battle. Sometimes, many slaves were sacrificed at the same time to stop a terrible disaster such as a severe **drought** or flood.

Humans who were sacrificed were killed with a sharp, sacrificial knife. Others might be killed by an arrow to their heart, by having their head cut off or by being thrown off the side of a high cliff. Some unfortunate victims died slowly as their skin was stripped from their body.

Sculptures such as this were meant to show the dead carrying offerings to the gods in the bowl on their chest.

Sacrifices to Chac, the Mayan god of rain, were made by throwing victims into sinkholes. These are deep wells created when underground streams made cave roofs collapse. The Maya believed these holes were a direct route to some of their gods.

KILLER FACT!

Some sacrificial knives were made from obsidian. Obsidian could be made into sharper blades than steel.

Glassy obsidian rock forms from volcanic lava as it cools. The rock was sharpened into a blade.

Bloody ball games

Mayan ball games involved death and offerings of blood. Some games re-enacted a battle between gods of the day and night, or good and evil. The losing players lost more than the game – they were killed.

Mayan ball games were played on a large court with two sloping walls opposite one another. Two teams passed a large ball to each other using only their knees, elbows or hips. A point was scored by getting the ball through a stone ring set high on the court walls.

Mayan ball courts were usually built at the base of a temple because the games were held in honour of the gods.

Warriors often played ball games against prisoners of war they had captured. The winners of the game were treated as heroes and given a great feast. The leader from the losing team, usually an important enemy ruler, was sacrificed to the gods.

DEADLY DID YOU KNOW?
After the leader of the losing team was sacrificed, his skull was used as the centre around which a new ball was made.

It was difficult to bounce a ball through stone hoops on the high walls without using hands.

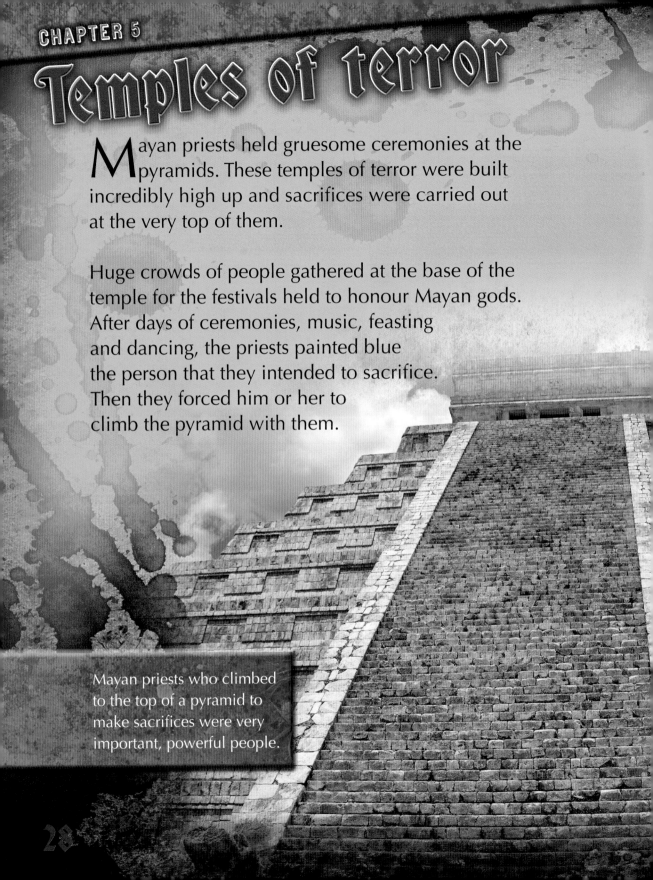

CHAPTER 5

Temples of terror

Mayan priests held gruesome ceremonies at the pyramids. These temples of terror were built incredibly high up and sacrifices were carried out at the very top of them.

Huge crowds of people gathered at the base of the temple for the festivals held to honour Mayan gods. After days of ceremonies, music, feasting and dancing, the priests painted blue the person that they intended to sacrifice. Then they forced him or her to climb the pyramid with them.

Mayan priests who climbed to the top of a pyramid to make sacrifices were very important, powerful people.

The pyramids used for ceremonies had two to four sets of steep staircases all the way to the top. As priests climbed up the high steps, they left Earth behind and moved towards the sky. They believed that this brought them and their sinister sacrifices closer to the gods.

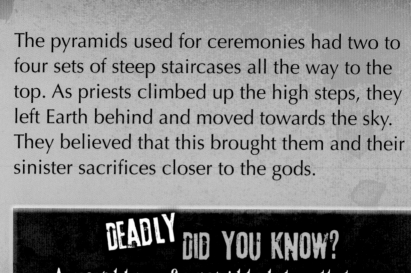

DEADLY DID YOU KNOW?

A second type of pyramid had steps that were almost too steep to climb. This type of temple was sacred and not meant to be touched. These pyramids often had secret tunnels, traps and doorways that led to dead ends.

This pyramid temple had an ancient Mayan ruler buried within it.

Platforms of fear

Sacrifices were made at special ceremonies on the large, flat platforms at the top of the high pyramids. The priests wore fierce-looking costumes and the huge crowds of people below watched them in fear and awe.

The priest led the victim to a stone **altar** on the temple platform. Helpers held down the victim while the priest quickly cut open his or her chest with a ceremonial knife. The priest removed the victim's heart while it was still beating.

The Maya believed that sacrifices held on these platforms of fear fed the gods and made sure the world would survive.

The victim's blood was then smeared onto an image of the god. The victim's body was often hurled down the temple steps where assistant priests removed its skin. A high priest then often wore the skin of the victim and performed a ritual dance in it.

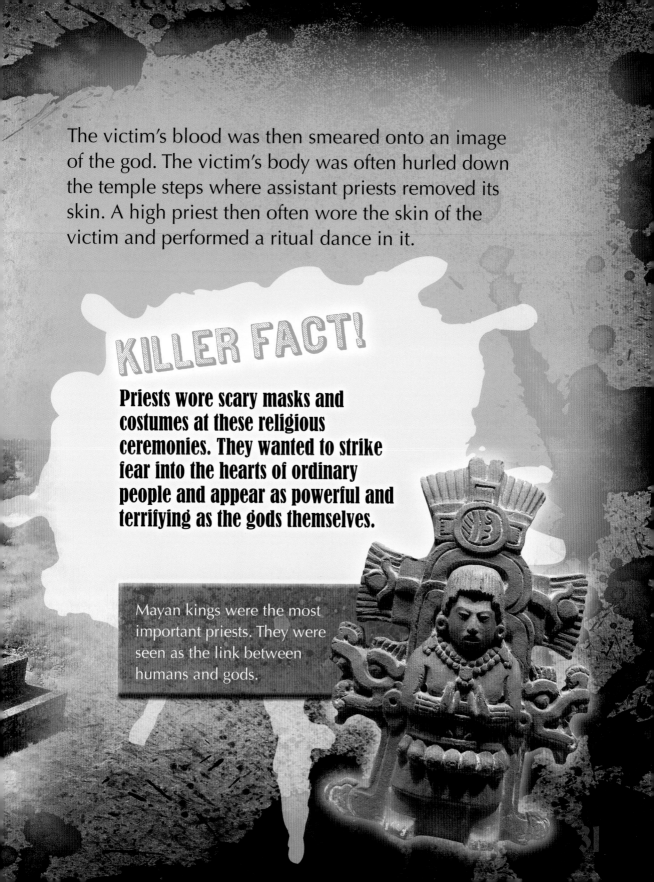

KILLER FACT!

Priests wore scary masks and costumes at these religious ceremonies. They wanted to strike fear into the hearts of ordinary people and appear as powerful and terrifying as the gods themselves.

Mayan kings were the most important priests. They were seen as the link between humans and gods.

Racks of skulls

The skulls of people who had been sacrificed were often placed on display in racks outside the temples. Some temples had stone carvings of these gruesome skull racks outside.

After a sacrifice, priests used their sharp obsidian knives to cut away the skin and muscles from a murdered victim, leaving only the skull. Then, they carved large holes in the sides of the skull so it could be attached to a thick wooden post.

The Maya believed that people who were sacrificed in these cruel ceremonies went straight to heaven.

Rows of skulls formed enormous racks in front of a temple or near a ball court. The losers of ball games were often beheaded and had their skulls placed on the skull rack, too. Sometimes, the skulls were piled one on top of another along tall vertical posts.

KILLER FACT!

Skull racks were built to show off how many enemies had been killed in a war, to deter enemies or to celebrate and commemorate those killed in sacrifice to the gods.

The Mayan rulers also used skull racks to terrify ordinary people into obeying them.

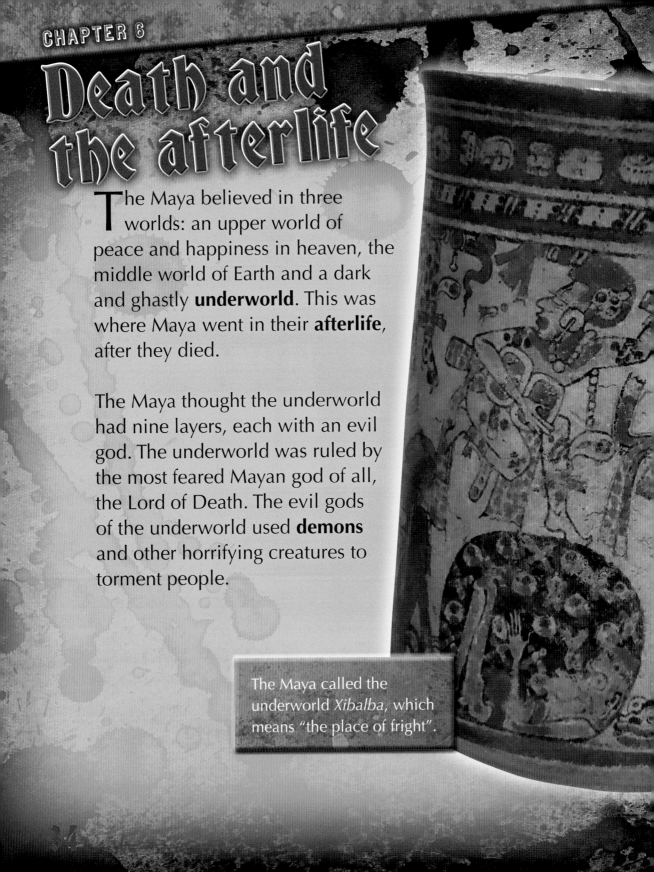

CHAPTER 6

Death and the afterlife

The Maya believed in three worlds: an upper world of peace and happiness in heaven, the middle world of Earth and a dark and ghastly **underworld**. This was where Maya went in their **afterlife**, after they died.

The Maya thought the underworld had nine layers, each with an evil god. The underworld was ruled by the most feared Mayan god of all, the Lord of Death. The evil gods of the underworld used **demons** and other horrifying creatures to torment people.

The Maya called the underworld *Xibalba*, which means "the place of fright".

The cruel demons and monsters of the underworld forced dead Maya to undergo terrifying tests of courage and skill. Maya who survived this dangerous place and its demons would be allowed to go to heaven forever more.

DEADLY DID YOU KNOW?
The macabre challenges the Maya faced in the underworld included a river of poisonous scorpions, killer jaguars and a game played with balls made of turning blades.

The demons of the underworld could cause pain, disease, starvation and even transform skeletons.

Living with the dead

When most ordinary Maya died, they were wrapped in a simple cotton cloth and buried beneath the floors of their house. This meant that for most Maya, the house that they lived in was both a family home and a **tomb**.

Before burial, relatives would paint the body with a red mineral called cinnabar. Red was the colour of death and rebirth for the Maya, so they often covered graves with cinnabar, too.

Some Maya were burned and their ashes put in urns like this one before burial.

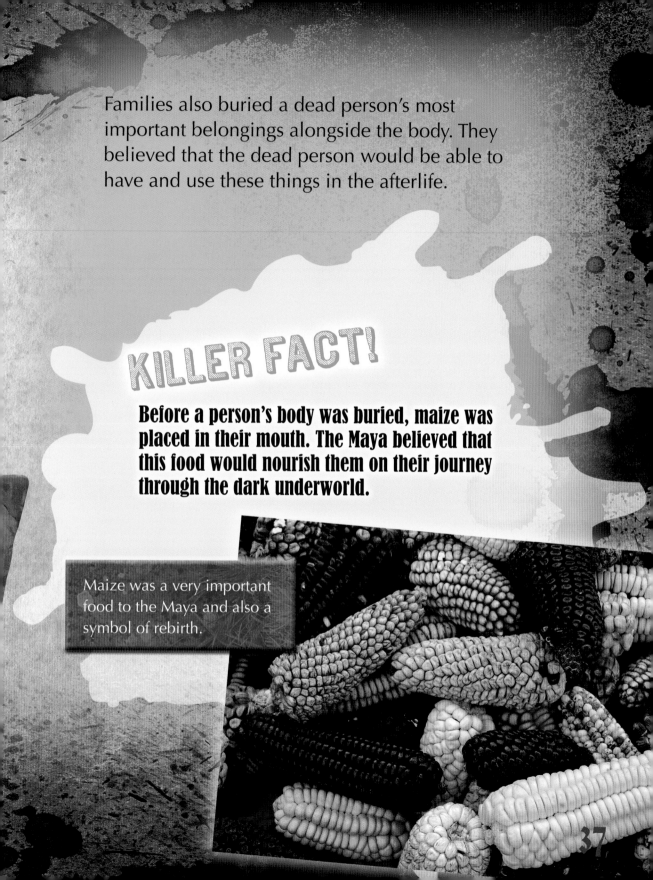

Families also buried a dead person's most important belongings alongside the body. They believed that the dead person would be able to have and use these things in the afterlife.

KILLER FACT!

Before a person's body was buried, maize was placed in their mouth. The Maya believed that this food would nourish them on their journey through the dark underworld.

Maize was a very important food to the Maya and also a symbol of rebirth.

Pleasing the dead

Burying dead relatives under a house may sound creepy, but it gave the Maya great comfort. They believed that burying their relatives under their house allowed their **ancestors** to watch over them and help to keep them safe.

The Maya had many traditions to remember relatives who had died. They regularly put offerings near where their loved ones were buried. They usually left these offerings several times a year, during feasts and on festival days.

When a house became damaged, Mayan families sometimes abandoned it, but still treated the house with the same respect as they would a tomb. The family would return to the house to give offerings to the dead.

This carving shows the god Itzamna on the right, whom the Maya believed could bring the dead back to life.

DEADLY DID YOU KNOW?

The Maya feared that if they did not please the gods, the gods would release the demons from the underworld. Then the demons would attack and destroy them. They hoped that by worshipping their ancestors, the ancestors would help prevent this.

The Maya usually left food and objects related to the dead relative's former life as offerings at their grave sites.

Terrible tombs

While ordinary people were buried under houses, Mayan kings were laid to rest in special tombs, often under their palaces or in giant pyramids. These tombs held some dark secrets.

Mayan kings were often buried in small rooms inside the pyramid. Their tombs were beautifully decorated and filled with treasures such as pendants made from gold and rare gemstones. These were for the king to use in the afterlife.

A king's prized possessions were often placed in his grave alongside his body.

When a king died, he did not travel to the afterlife alone. Unfortunate members of the royal family or court officials were often sacrificed so they could accompany him. Slaves were also killed when their owners died, so that they could continue their service after death.

DEADLY DID YOU KNOW?

Regular offerings were left to dead kings at the royal tombs. It is also believed that living rulers used bloodletting rituals to contact specific ancestors from their royal family to ask them for help.

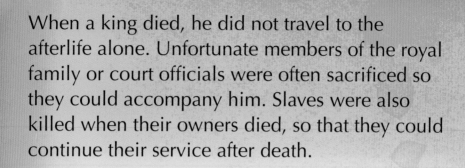

Inside a king's tomb, there were other chambers where those sacrificed could join him in the afterlife.

Masks of death

The Maya believed that when a mighty and powerful king died, he would become a god. That is why kings were buried with their faces covered by spooky-looking death masks.

Death masks were often made to look like a king when he was alive. They were usually made from the rare green stone, jade. This was the most sacred and precious of all materials in the Mayan world.

This is the jade burial mask of Pakal the Great, king of the city of Palenque, who ruled from the age of twelve to eighty.

The Maya believed that an expensive and elaborate death mask would prove to the gods that the dead person was an important king when he arrived in the underworld. The mask would help the gods of the underworld recognize him and treat him as another god.

KILLER FACT!

When a king or official died, priests pried open his mouth and put a jade bead inside. The Maya believed that the jade would help the corpse breathe again and come back from the dead.

For the Maya, jade was a symbol of eternal life.

Death of the Maya

The murderous Maya ruled over their bloodthirsty civilization from about AD 300 to 900. Then their cities were abandoned and the Maya were gone.

Some experts think that a deadly disease wiped out most of the Maya. It also seems likely that many people in Mayan cities were killed in violent attacks from other cities or by **invaders** from other lands.

Mayapán, the last great city of the Maya, was surrounded by a high wall to protect it from deadly attacks.

The Maya may have brought about their own end by their farming methods. They burned down trees to clear land for farming. Over time, this damaged the soil and made it useless for growing **crops**. In the end, perhaps many Maya fled the region to find new land that they could farm and live on.

DEADLY DID YOU KNOW?

Some scientists say that a terrible drought struck at this time. With no rain, plants did not grow and there was nothing to drink. Perhaps the unfortunate Maya slowly starved to death.

Among the only traces of the Mayan civilization are crumbling stone carvings to remind us of its ancient glories and its horror stories.

Glossary

afterlife life after death. Some people believe that after we die we go to live in another world.

altar table or platform on which religious rituals are carried out

ancestors relatives who have died

civilization settled community in which people live together and use systems such as writing to communicate

corpse dead body

crops plants grown for food

demons evil spirits or devils

drought period of time with little or no rainfall

evil spirits dangerous supernatural beings

flooding when water covers an area of land that is usually dry

humiliated made to feel embarrassed or foolish

invaders people, armies or countries that use force to enter and take control of another country

macabre gruesome

monument statue, building or other structure made to remember an event, time or person

mythical something from a traditional, well-known, but made-up, story

nobles people in the highest class in certain societies

obsidian hard, dark, glass-like volcanic rock

offering something that people give as part of a religious ceremony or ritual

predator animal that kills other animals for food

priests religious leaders

quarry open mine

rainforests thick forests of tall trees found in wet, tropical areas

ritual ceremony performed for religious reasons

sacred important to a religion

sacrifices animals or humans killed to honour a god or gods

slaves people who are owned by other people and must obey them

symbol image that represents something else

tear gas gas that burns the eyes and makes them water

temples buildings that people visit to worship their god or gods

tomb building where dead people are laid to rest

tribute gift of food or other items paid by people to their ruler

underworld mythical world of the dead

venomous poisonous

Find out more

Books

Daily Life in the Maya Civilization (Daily Life in Ancient Civilizations), Nick Hunter (Raintree, 2016)

DKfindout! Maya, Incas and Aztecs, DK (DK Children, 2018)

The Maya (Great Civilisations), Tracey Kelly (Franklin Watts, 2015)

Mayan Civilisation (Explore!), Izzi Howell (Wayland, 2018)

The Mayans (History Hunters), Louise Spilsbury (Raintree, 2016)

Websites

www.bbc.com/bitesize/articles/zg2htv4
Learn what life was like for the Maya.

www.dkfindout.com/uk/history/mayans
Find out more about the Maya.

Index